Essay

MW01241278

Parts I-VI and Part VII

The Collection

and

Class Warfare

by John David

Cover by Christine Ticali

johndavidauthor.com

ISBN: 1475111355

ASIN: B007JNHTZU

Also in audiobook and ebook versions

V. 4 of a series

Table of Contents

Part I

The Carrot and The Stick

Most people clearly understand the concept of rewarding good behavior, and punishing the bad. Most animals do as well, which is why we use the "stick" to punish them, and the "carrot" to reward them, when we are trying to "train" them to act a certain way. Yet somehow, when it comes to the average American's relationship with their government, all we ever seem to receive is the stick, at least on the most visible, immediate level.

Can't pay your taxes? Lose your home.

Drive without car insurance? Lose your car.

Stand up for your beliefs? Lose your freedom.

There are countless examples of this kind of punitive relationship we have with our governments, on all levels, in every state across this great country of ours.

That's right, I said *our* country. It does not belong to the past—the past is dead. It does not belong to the future, that does not yet exist. Our country belongs to us, the 99%, the Americans who are alive in it, right here, right now.

We are the heart, the soul, and the backbone of this great Nation.

For too long, we have been asked to sacrifice, to postpone, to be patient, to suffer in silence, while the 1% do nothing of the sort. They gleefully frolic and wallow in excess, while we, the democratic majority, sometimes must decide between food this week, and gas next week. **It is difficult to understand and accept why we must sacrifice our present *and* our future, while they do neither.**

It is truly a noble aspiration to consider the price of our actions that must be paid by future generations, but if there is no future but despair for us, that nobility will have been wasted.

I do not propose that we act blindly without consideration for the eventual consequences, only that we weigh in proper measure and proportion those actions to what has meaning *now*, versus the unknown, "eventual" future that may, or may not be.

If there is no next month for us, there will be no next year, and so on.

If we can so clearly see that the result of our "negative," anti-social behavior is punishment and condemnation by our society and our government, why then is it so hard to find any value in "righteousness" and good citizenship?

How is it that the most the "good-hearted" citizen can expect from their government for years of doing right, paying taxes, and obeying

laws, is simply and only to *not* be beaten with the stick?

Would it not be much more effective on every level if in fact a citizen could expect *rewards* for doing that which is good, as well as punishment for that which is bad? Is this not how we teach our children? "Clean your room and we will go get ice-cream," seems to be much more effective in motivating "right" behavior than does "Don't clean your room, and you will be grounded!"

We understand this instinctively when relating to children, and even animals, yet somehow we expect adults to forget the blissful pleasure of the rewards for good behavior, and only to know and respect the fear of the consequences of non-compliance.

How stupidly regressive and backwards thinking is this flawed, unnatural philosophy of implementing "order" in our modern society. How awful it is and has been, for so long, to have nothing to look forward to for a *lifetime* of compliance and right action, but the prospect of *not* being punished?

Would it not be exponentially more effective and gratifying, to see the rewards of right thinking, right action, right-being, immediately, in the form of rewards for that behavior we as a society wish to encourage?

Stay out of jail for a year? Reward.

Stay employed for a year? Reward.

Pay your taxes on time and in full? Reward.

Of course, by "rewards," I do not necessarily mean "money." Some will say:

"We can't afford to pay people to do what they should just rightfully do anyway!"

Maybe not.

Maybe rewards have nothing to do with money, except where it is determined that money is the proper and best motivator of the behavior we wish to encourage.

Maybe prestige is what works best. Perhaps a better parking space? Who can say? Has anyone asked *you* lately what would make you feel better about doing what you already do without recognition or reward? Most likely it is different things to different people, but there are no doubt some common threads of reason that can be found to bind and positively reinforce that which we seek to encourage. A way to link desirable behavior to real, tangible, and understandable rewards that can be achieved and enjoyed here, in the now.

What is needed is a real quantum shift in political philosophy, from the useless and

ineffective models of the past, to new, exciting, and engaging theories of the now.

For too long, the country has been *owned* and run by those who have only their best interests in mind. **Regardless of party, our government has been captured by everyone *but* the people.** When was the last time you woke up thinking that *your* government was putting your interests first?

Can't remember, can you? Because they don't, because they haven't, <u>because they won't until you force them to remember who, and what, the country really is</u>:

It is you, it is me, and it is *us*. Without "the people" there is no country.

Stop living in fear. Stop hiding your distaste for what you know is wrong. Speak out.

Join the free citizens of the greatest country history has ever known in taking back the freedom from fear.

Join the 99% who are the heart, the soul, and the backbone of this great Nation.

Become a supporter of the 99%, and I promise you, your voice will be heard.

Thanks for listening.

Part II

A Call to Action

In Part I, I discussed some ideas about who our government represents, and what it is and does.

I also described the broken, dysfunctional relationship that most Americans have with that system, and some ideas for reformation. With that said:

What can, or should our government be and do for loyal, hardworking, good-hearted citizens?

Good question.

Government should be the reliable, faithful, loyal servant and confidant of the people.

Government should not be feared, but respected.

Citizens who fear their leadership may be controlled, but they will *never* be loyal.

Loyal citizens will fight and die for country and citizenship.

How can citizens trust a government that they fear?

Yet the 1% now extract the very lifeblood of the people, via force and threats, all the while claiming that any change or modification to the "system" would cause catastrophic collapse.

Would it really? I think not.

I think that the fear of change, real change, is the foremost and only threat to our great society and nation. Things have been done the same way, by the same people, for so long, that the concept of change has become some foreign idea. Yet if viewed from a biological perspective, growth, evolution, and change is not only necessary, but desirable for a living organism to both survive and prosper.

What is human society, if not a living organism? Should not our governments, then, reflect the composition and order of the society they allegedly represent? Why is the idea of true "proportional representation" such a foreign and repulsive concept?

It is so because it has been presented that way, by the traitors of our culture, the whores who have sold themselves and their integrity, for little more than money. When the love of self, of money, of things, has become more important than the love of country, of neighbor, of those NOT the self, then it is time for these so-called "leaders" of our country to *go*.

Traitor is a very strong word, and I use it purposefully, with clear intention. Look it up. If you betray your country, your friends, yourself, for nothing more than money, what else could you possibly be called, if not a traitor?

You are certainly not an idealist, or a patriot.

Those are words reserved for people with actual principles, who serve something other than the simple physical needs of the self, glorified by pure lucre and the "rewards" it brings.

I have long proposed that those who *want* to be leaders of our society, most likely should not be allowed to be so. Why would any "rational" person spend 100 million dollars or more, to be "elected" to a job that pays 250k a year? Does that make any sense to you? Desire is the root of destruction. Those who want to lead may not be the best choices for that role.

We would almost certainly be no worse off, and would most likely be better off, simply shanghaiing people right from corners, bus stops, coffee shops, or classrooms, and "appointing" them as leaders.

At the very least this would ensure that our "representatives" are in fact that, a representation of whom and what we are, rather than some fractional slice of what we wish we could be, that is, rich, indolent, and indifferent to the concerns of anyone but ourselves.

In times of war, the idea of conscripting soldiers to "defend" our nation with their lives, blood, and limbs, is somehow perfectly acceptable, yet the concept of doing the same to "enlist" leaders who might even actually keep the nation *out* of wars, is again, something foreign and repugnant to us?

Why might that be? Who stands to lose the most from such a "revolutionary" program?

Tabula Rasa is my proposal. Nothing less. Throw the bums out. All of them.

Why do the sheeple of this nation cry and whine for "change" while continuing to "elect" the very same "leaders" who have so clearly failed to do anything reminiscent of that title? When did the concept of public service and sacrifice evolve into the unholy corruption of "government" we are subjected to now?

To be fair, it is not all the fault of our leaders.

They did not all start out as they have become.

Some of them actually had ideals and principles, even dreams, once. But, as it is said, when you lie down with dogs, you will wake up with fleas. We expect too much from that rare individual actually capable of enacting change. We toss them into the political pool, and simply add bricks until they either drown, or are "saved" by someone much less ethical than themselves.

Then we act "surprised" when they fail to become anything better than the scum that surrounds them.

Democracy, it seems, simply does not work. Why should it? We expect too much from "mob rule." The so-called Representative Republic concept, also seems a colossal failure, in that we are neither representative, nor a republic.

Sometimes we can solve the problems of the present by learning from the lessons of the past.

Control of government should be evolutionary in nature and purpose, responding to the needs and desires of the governed, in accordance with the capabilities of society and economy. Even a child understands that you simply cannot have everything that you want. You cannot be all things to all people, and if indeed you are that, surely you have failed at true "leadership."

In the end, it all boils down to "desire."

Do we want to change? Do we want things to be better, or even different than they are today, or than they have been in the past? If so, are we willing to pay the true cost of that choice? Or are we in fact the lowest form of coward, that which is unwilling even to risk the smallest loss? Ask yourself that question.

What kind of American am I?

Is my own life and security worth more than the life and security of the nation, and the future?

If you answer yes, then you are in effect saying that your children, and their children, are on their own—that your needs and desires of today are worth more than those of tomorrow. Anyone making this choice should carefully consider the implications. To do nothing today is a tacit acceptance of tomorrow's status quo.

I expect more than this from the 99%, the good-hearted people of America.

But I understand fear. I have been taught to fear many things by the society in which we live. Fear of poverty. Fear of war. Fear of the unknown, the "other," the "enemy" of the day or week. Fear is a reality, it is unavoidable, even useful. That is where "courage" comes in. Courage is not, as some believe, defined as the absence of fear.

Rather, it is the willingness to take action despite fear, to run *towards* the fire, instead of away, because you know that there are those at risk who may suffer and die if you do not.

Now is that time that we all must be accountable for what we have *not* done.

The failure to act is at least as heinous of a crime as wrong action itself. There is no more time for inaction. Our future as a nation, a people, a free race is at stake.

Once again, "election season" is upon us.

Will you continue to "flip a coin" and anoint "heads" or "tails" to "lead" us?

It is time to elect "silver dollars" to lead this great nation. We have had leadership by "quarters" and "dimes" for too long.

"Republican," or "Democrat."

Heads or tails, a dime is a dime, and a quarter is a quarter. They represent the same thing.

Not enough.

Choose more.

Step up.

Be bold.

"Waste" your vote.

Your neighbor is not your enemy.

The traitors of our culture, our way of life . . . they are the enemy.

They smile and ask you to sacrifice your job, your comfort, your way of life . . . while they profit from your despair.

Your children ask you "Why?"

And you cannot answer them.

Fear is your enemy. Courage is your friend.

What kind of American are you?

This November, ask yourself that question.

When you vote . . . answer it.

Thanks for listening.

Part III

The Auction

In Part II, I left you with "A Call to Action," regarding the upcoming "election" we are about to have. In that election, if nothing changes, we will once again elect either "heads" (the incumbent Democrat) or "tails" (the "winner" of the nomination process), or as I like to say, the "highest bidder" amongst the field of Republican candidates.

The title of this essay is *The Auction*, and I chose that name because that is effectively what our electoral process has become. The player names will change, but the game remains the same.

This time around, a Republican will be nominated to oppose a Democrat, as if it really matters which face the millionaire wears. A, B, C, or D, they all have one very important trait in common, that is, they are *nothing* like you and me, the 99%.

As I write, literally hundreds of millions of dollars, if not *billions*, are being spent in pursuit of being anointed the "winning" candidate. How odd is this "democratic" system of "government" that we now have, whereby whoever has the most gold, wins? How much farther from the founder's intentions can this process possibly be?

The saddest, most terrible part of this whole dog and pony show is that, in the end, there will be no "winner" for the American people, the 99% of this Nation who are the heart, the soul, and the backbone of our society.

There will be only losers, and they will be us.

We will all be losers, as yet another millionaire buys the crown, and therefore the right to "lead" us even farther down the path of destruction. More jobs will be sent overseas, more foreign wars enacted, more homes foreclosed upon, and more families torn apart, simply so that we can say we let this so-called "democratic process" work again.

Would it not be so much more effective, honest, and beneficial for the nation, for us all, if we simply held one huge, final "Auction" the night before the election in November, whereby each candidate simply "bid" as much as they and their puppeteers were willing to pay each of us for our vote?

Instead of spending those hundreds of millions, and billions, on attack and smear ads, stupid campaign posters, flyers, and other political refuse, we simply allowed our masters to pay us directly for the office of President, and for all political offices?

The other day I actually heard one of those simpleton commentators employed by a "news" network actually say as much, regarding the Republican nomination process.

"Candidate A is spending umpty dollars per vote received, whereas Candidate B has spent umpty dollars plus ten!" she enthused, never once opining that there could not possibly be a clearer picture of the fatal virus that infects our electoral process, than the statement she had just made.

As I said, if this is how we are to determine our rulers and leaders, then let them give us the money directly. I for one can certainly use the cash. We as voters should be able to simply go online, register to "vote," and list our vote for sale to the highest bidder, eBay style. The more conscientious of us would of course set a high reserve, because God forbid that we sell our right of self-determination too cheaply.

Candidates could then login to the "Auction," and instantly determine how much will be needed to buy the current election, with all of the proceeds actually going to the "voters," instead of the pundits, commentators, spin doctors, and other non-essential election service providers. If we ran our elections this way, at least the process would be "honest," without the "candidates" needing to maintain the pretense of having any desire to become a "public servant," thereby interfering with the transaction we are enacting.

We "the people" would also be spared the charade of pretending that "heads" actually was better than "tails," and that was why we "voted" for them. Realistically, in the last few auctions, er, elections, we have really not voted *for* the "better" candidate, we have voted *against* the more awful one.

Imagine this more perfect political climate. There would be no campaign signs mucking up the landscape, no ads blaring "heads is worse than tails, by far!" cluttering up our airwaves, our minds, and polluting our eyeballs, forcing us to engage in fruitless water-cooler chats over whether "heads" or "tails" is the better choice this time around.

You see, "The Auction" really is the best policy, isn't it? What better sign of commitment can a millionaire or billionaire possibly make to the 99%, besides demonstrating the willingness to spend a sizeable portion of their largesse to buy the right to lead you?

Are you not entertained by this circus?

But now, you say, I am offending you.

"How dare you imply that I would simply 'sell' my vote to the highest bidder? I am an educated, honorable American citizen!"

Are you really?

What makes you believe that? What have you done to demonstrate that you have any actual principles that have not been "force-fed" to you by the overlords of our society? Politically speaking, have you ever taken a real stand for anything?

Be honest.

You are afraid to.

You have listened to those who have warned you against "wasting your vote," by actually using it for its intended purpose, that is, to reflect your political will, and the will of the people of this great nation.

Instead, every election, you actually *have* wasted that vote, by refusing to even consider that someone who has *not* spent umpty million dollars **might actually be the most worthy, and the best leader we could ever possibly find.**

Don't you know that this great nation was founded in defiance of the "Divine Right" of kings? That the founders specifically repudiated the idea that money and power should have anything to do with determining the right to rule the people?

Have you ever actually read the *Declaration of Independence*?

Why not?

Maybe you should.

I'll help you out a little. Here we go:

We hold these truths to be self-evident, (that means, "So blatantly obvious that further explanation is unnecessary").

That ALL men (and women, emphasis and paraphrase mine) *are entitled to life, liberty, and the pursuit of happiness.*

That to secure these rights, governments are instituted among Men, <u>deriving their just powers from the consent of the governed</u>, (that means you have agreed to this!).

That whenever any Form of Government becomes destructive of these ends, <u>it is the Right of the People to alter or abolish it</u>, and to institute new Government . . .

Does this ring any bells? Have you "consented" to this? If so, please stop reading now, because this essay is not for you. You already have what you have paid for.

If not, by all means, continue reading.

This essay is for you, the 99%, the heart, the soul, and the backbone of this great Nation.

The gal who pours your coffee every morning, the guy who dumps your trash every week, the flat-footed cop on the beat, the teacher of your children, all of whom do what they do every day, never expecting that they will receive anything that they do not deserve, that they have not worked for, and earned, they are the ones that I write this essay for.

I care not for the millionaires and billionaires, the 1% who are the "owners" of this nation.

I will not mourn their passing, nor should you.

They have had their reward, and their chance to do what was right.

They simply chose not to do it.

Regarding the 1%, I have only this to say:

You *will* be held accountable.

For every job you sent overseas, so you could get *another* million in your annual bonus, for the blood money you took for your disloyalty and betrayal of our nation, our people, of our way of life.

"Free Trade." What a cruel joke. What did you trade our way of life for?

Money, and nothing else. Certainly not idealism, or patriotism.

For every "Joe Sixpack" trying to explain to his children that "we have to move now, because we can't afford our house anymore," as he died a little inside, that is also on you.

For every broken man or woman, lying in some ditch somewhere, mumbling to themselves, remembering what they used to have, or do, their misery is upon you.

You put them there. Are you proud? Are you fulfilled?

This was your neighbor, your friend, the guy you went to high school with, the gal at your senior prom.

The proud men and women of this great Nation, who built a fledgling democracy from the ground up, **who planted our flag on the Moon**, and built roads, bridges, and monuments to Democracy, because they believed in the "American Dream," who now despair because they cannot provide for their children, their misery is also upon you.

You should be ashamed.

You have everything that you need, plus more. They have nothing, not even dreams. You took those away from them too, you sold them to the highest bidder, overseas, to some foreigner who, like you, delighted in their despair.

Are you happy now? Are you a "success?"

Are you a "patriot?"

I think not.

Do you feel pride in the misery you have created? Will your money comfort you in the next life, as it has in this one? Consider that question most carefully, for "the ears of the Lord are open to the prayers of the righteous," **and most certainly that is not you.**

The price of your betrayal *will* be paid.

For the rest of us, the 99%, we must also accept some responsibility for letting this happen, because we stood by and watched, and did nothing, even though many of us knew we were being led down a path of destruction. We have watched for years as political offices were bought and sold to the highest bidder. We watched those leaders dance on the strings of their masters, as we let "quarters," and "dimes" rule us.

I for one would rather have a new, clean, "Liberty" dollar leading this nation. Someone nobody has ever heard of. A person who has spent their whole life in the service of those around them, as they quietly and efficiently did the right thing, without ever being asked or paid to do so. Perhaps that person is reading this essay right now, and humbly thinking to themselves, "He's right! We really do need someone just like that person, whoever they are!"

The goal of this essay was to provide you with some clarity—to help you see things as they actually are. The choice really is very simple.

This November, you will be asked to "give" away your vote, to "heads" or "tails," without payment. Or, you will be told repeatedly, by pundits and perhaps even by your "friends," you can "waste" your vote, and use it to actually express your democratic will.

Which will you choose?

Remember, you will not be paid, for "giving" your vote to heads or tails.

Ask yourself this question:

If I "win" this election (that is, my candidate spends more to "buy" it), what will I, my family, my friends, and my neighbors have "won?"

Anything?

When I wake up, the "morning after," will I feel regret? Will I want to chew my arm off for casting that "vote?"

Or will I feel pride?

Pride because I took the path *less* traveled by?

The one that has made "all the difference?"

Choose wisely.

Thanks for listening.

Part IV

The Choice

In Part III, I asked you to "choose wisely" in the upcoming election cycle. I also talked about some of the reasons why we would want to "waste" our votes, or at the very least, honestly sell them at a fair price.

Keep in mind, my purpose is, and always will be, what is best for us, and for the Nation. The selfish focus on the individual, on profit, and on largesse has been our downfall, and it is what has brought us to this point in the first place.

I am not promoting Socialism, or any sort of "revolution" to that purpose. My goal is the reformation of our culture and our society, so that it is forced to evolve into something more closely resembling what the founders intended it to be.

To do that, we must first find that common ground, a place from which legitimate discussion can begin. We must accept the truth.

Very few will disagree with the idea that the system we have in place to establish and lead our government is broken and dysfunctional. Even the 1% will tell you that, as they gleefully work to overcome the few remaining obstacles to their perfect corruption of our society.

They seek what is essentially a return to feudalism and serfdom for us all, whereby the fruits of our daily labors are barely sufficient to sustain us, and any surplus created by that labor accrues solely and entirely to them.

In their more perfect world, they will own everything, from the ground we stand on, to the water we drink, and indeed the very air we breathe. Rest assured, they will find a way to sell you that air, once they have polluted the "free" air to the point that it is no longer safe enough to breathe.

When you wake up one day, and begin to write out your check to the local "Air Company," remember that I told you so.

Remember also how you laughed in disbelief at the very thought of that coming to pass, as your parents did at the idea that we would one day pay for the water we drink—yet here we are.

It is said that one of the definitions of "insanity" is the mindless repetition of the same fruitless act, over and over again, hoping and predicting that the outcome will somehow, one day, magically be different from the thousand days before it.

Are we then, insane?

Is not our continued vain attempt at finding leadership and reformation from amongst the ranks of the same two failed parties who now own and run the political structure of this country, by this definition, insane? Isn't more than fifty years of this enough to prove to you that it is in fact, impossible, unlikely, and indeed *madness* to expect any real deviation from the path of failure we are on now, if we do not ever choose to depart from it?

Think about that for one moment. How can we continue to be "surprised" by the Sun's continued insistence on rising in the east, and setting in the west, merely because every morning we stare and predict with certainty that it will not? That *this* morning will be different, *this* time the sun will rise in the north, and set in the south, and all will be well, and different.

But we know that will not happen.

We know that it is dark at night, and light in the day. We know that we breathe air, and not water. So simple are these facts of existence that to even debate them invites ridicule, yet somehow, vehement discussions of the superiority of "heads" over "tails" take place every day, throughout this land, by "educated" and "informed" individuals, not just by children and idiots, from whom we might expect this kind of babbling disillusionment.

Indeed, we often find ourselves engaged in these types of lame discussions, as if no viable alternatives to this predictable "insanity" even existed.

My fellow Americans, my friends, the 99% of you who are the heart, the soul, and the backbone of this great Nation, I assure you, such a path away from madness, towards the light at the end of the tunnel, does indeed exist.

I have seen it.

It is a world designed with digital evolution, not analog decay and stagnation. It is a country filled with dreams, and dreamers, artists, musicians, athletes, scientists, and builders of all the things that have made this nation greater than any other in the history of the world. I feel so strongly about that phrase, that I will repeat it for you.

"A nation greater than any other in the history of the world."

How long has it been since you felt the natural pride that you *should* feel from being a part and party to that greatness? Since you looked around you, at your neighbors, your friends, your family, and said to yourself, "we are the envy of all the world, they hate us for our beauty and our art, for our compassion and great works, which stand as shining beacons of righteousness to every land?"

It's been a while, hasn't it?

You see, the 1% have taken even what little we had left from us, that is, our pride.

The products of our minds and hands slip into obscurity amongst those of other nations, as we fall from our lofty perch of eminence to second, and ultimately third-class status amongst our peers.

This is the greatest crime of all. The greatest theft of all.

The loss of our dreams, our passion, our pride at the fruits of our labors, such that we hate the very work we do, and those we do it with. We no longer love our neighbors, we do not rely on them, or trust them, and in fact many of us cannot even name the people who live on either side of us.

Why might that be?

Do you think that this is a normal human condition, or the right way to live, in any society? Remember back to your childhood. I for one could name the folks across and down the street from me, as well as those who lived beside us. I knew and cared that they were safe and secure in their homes, and that their children were as well.

Yet look at us now, we stare and glare at our neighbors for parking in "our" spot, for mowing 4" of our lawn, for allowing their delinquent children to toss a ball into our yards. **God forbid that any of them should take from us what little we have left.**

As I said, there is a way back from this condition, a return to "sanity," if you will. But we have to *want* to get better, and if indeed we do, the rest will be easy. Once we make and accept the choice of taking a different path, clearly and obviously the destination we arrive at will also be different, and in this case, we already know, with utmost certainty, that the road to "more of the same," leads to nowhere that we have not already been before, and nowhere that we actually want to go.

This is the hardest part of our "recovery."
Acknowledging that we have a problem, and then choosing to get better. Once we make that choice, the rest will be easy. If we know with utter certainty that Plan "A" is a fail plan, knowledge we have gained from years of attempting and failing at it, why on earth would any rational person choose to take that same path yet again?

Once we all have decided that we will no longer attempt Plan A, but are willing and devoted to implementing Plan "B," we will have taken that first giant step *back* towards sanity and reform.

My friends, Plan B will lead us to a brighter future, for it most certainly will not be more of the same. Very simply, if each and every one of us merely votes for something other than "heads" or "tails," actually votes their conscience, then no matter what the outcome, there are two things we can be sure of.

One, that **we will have left the known path of destruction**, and two, we will have set out upon a path to a *different* destination, and that our leaders, whoever they may be, will not be beholden to any particular interest, but our own.

They will not have been bought and paid for, to such an extent that they are powerless to act in any way that is beneficial to us. Indeed, our current leaders no longer even remember how to be "public servants." We the people will have to learn who our new leaders are, and what they represent, and they will not have to unlearn treachery and corruption. They will be "blank slates" upon which we can write our will, the will of the people, not of the few, that the political needs of the many should be met.

The 1% can, and will always be able to take care of themselves. It is for ourselves only that we should be concerned at this point, nothing and no one else.

Not foreign affairs, or wars on foreign shores.

Not how quickly we can ship ever more of our jobs overseas, but how quickly we can bring them back home. Our focus should be on putting Americans to work fixing our problems, rather than on paying the people of other nations to exacerbate them.

Once we have chosen and enacted Plan B, we can begin the path to reformation and reform of our

society and culture, and regain our rightful,
preeminent place amongst the nations of the world.

**We cannot ask other nations to respect us, if we
do not respect ourselves.**

My friends, my brothers and sisters, the night after
election day, sleep peacefully.

Wake up to a brighter future.

Look into the mirror and be proud to say . . .

"I made the right choice."

Thanks for listening.

Part V

Plan B

In Part IV, I discussed the urgent necessity of implementing "Plan B" as a means of effecting reform and reconstruction of our political process, and of our society. The most important attribute of Plan B is primarily that it is *not* "Plan A," which is more of the same.

I also reminded you that what is needed is a new path a new course, with a brighter future, one that offers actual "hope" to you and me, not the **"faux hope"** propounded by the liars and violators of our freedoms and rights, who call themselves our "leaders" today. Real "hope" means having the knowledge that, with utmost certainty, the path we are on today is not the same fail path of yesterday. *Any* path not the path of "destruction," the fail path of Plan A, will be better.

You will not be "wasting" your vote by casting it in favor of your actual democratic will. To the contrary, you can be assured that it will be more effective than it has ever been before, because it will actually make a difference.

I guarantee it.

So what exactly is Plan B?

It is the brightly lit road to reform, and the restoration of the "true" path of democracy for this Nation, as the founders intended. I believe that our forefathers would weep for us, their metaphorical progeny, as we are abused by our present "rulers" with much greater fervor than King George was ever able to perpetrate against them.

Not only are we "taxed" without "real" representation, we are "surveilled," and "monitored" without probable cause, in direct violation of the *Bill of Rights*. King George could only dream of possessing the power that our current leaders have over us today, all in the name of "patriotism," and the prevention of "terrorism."

But who are the real "terrorists?"

Who wields the heavy "stick" against you more effectively, some dirty third-world thug in a cave half a world away, or "Big Brother," who reads your emails, tracks your library borrows and video rentals, and even tells you what name you may have? Have you heard of the so-called "Real ID" program? It is an unholy offspring of the "Patriot Act," whereby (among other things) your "name" is what the state says it is, not what you want it to be. It is also a direct violation of the Constitution, specifically the 10th Amendment, among others.

The present state of affairs in our nation breaks my heart, because I know that we are capable, and indeed are worthy of, so much more than this.

In less than a generation, look at how far we have fallen. Those of you who have been alive as long as I have, can remember when our dollar was worth "something," when our labor was worth something, when our machines and the products of that labor were also the best available, and the ones everyone wanted to have. In quick succession, all of those achievements became only memories, as our nation now ranks as among the "second-tier" countries of the world. Annual income, health care, infrastructure— the list of our "deficiencies" versus other nations goes on and on.

If our Nation was a cruise ship, a "vessel" if you will, and she had run aground, and was now floundering and sinking, whose fault would it be? The passengers? The crew? The cooks, the porters, the deckhands?

No. It would be the fault of the "captain," and to a lesser extent, all of the other officers, because they are the ones who set the course and speed, who decide to turn left or right, to stop, or to move forward. The passengers and crew have absolutely no say in those decisions, once they have made the choice to embark on that journey, with that ship and crew.

Now consider the direction our "Ship of State" is heading.

Do you believe it is on the right course? Do you have confidence in the captain, and in the officers?

Why not?

Because they have done nothing to inspire that confidence. For years now they have merely "circled the drain," economically speaking, with the best performances being by those "captains" who have not *lost* any ground, but simply held our position. The present captain and officers have been warned of "Icebergs ahead!" yet have chosen to maintain course, and even to increase the speed at which we head towards certain disaster.

Does this sound familiar? Almost like the plot of some movie.

And how did that story end, again?

Ship on the bottom of the ocean, bodies floating in the water . . . that's right, now I remember.

It wasn't exactly what anyone would call a happy ending.

Consider now the present course and speed of our Ship of State. We know that our captain and officers are incompetent. We *know* that they are lost, and have no idea how to get back "on course." We know this because we have given them chance after chance. We have repaired the ship time and time again, and handed it over to another set of officers, who have only repeated the grave mistakes of the previous ones. They have thrown their hands up in confusion, as they sound the alarm again and again, putting the passengers into a panicked state. They navigate in great circles, never making any progress, while loudly proclaiming that simply *not* sinking the ship is a victory of some kind.

Is it really?

I think not.

I believe with utmost certainty and complete conviction that it is time for a *new* captain and new officers. That there is not a single competent one amongst those we have now. If there are any, they have done nothing honorable or noteworthy, and are therefore as untrustworthy as the rest of the failed officers.

My friends, my brothers and sisters, the Ship of State is fine. She is battered, and her paint is not so glossy, but she is a sound vessel, and will take our Nation anywhere we want to go, in safety and comfort. The only thing she lacks is a *competent* complement of officers and crew, and a new navigational chart, that they may use to guide them to the correct destination.

We the "passengers" of that ship, have the ability to hire that new crew. We can do it anytime we choose.

But first, we must "fire" the old ones.

They are no longer worthy of our trust, our money, our lives and security. It is time for the 99% of this once greater Nation to step up and do *our* part, that is, to take responsibility for choosing competent leaders, and for giving them the "tools" that they need to actually take us where we want to go.

If I remove the "steering wheel" from an ancient Chevette, and replace it with a new "CTS-V" steering wheel, does that somehow transform the old beater into a Cadillac? Will it now "perform" like a sports car?

No.

Replacing the "steering wheel" of the failed party with another, "shiny" new one, does not change the fact that we are still driving the same old jalopy as before. Nor does it change the road we are on. Going to the "car lot" of democracy, selecting a "new" model, (one that we have *not* driven before), buying a "new" map, then embarking upon a path *not* traveled before . . . .

This is the recipe for reform, for the reconstruction of our failed democracy. Doing something, going somewhere, that we have not gone before. Do you understand? Is this clear enough for you?

You will not be wasting your vote, by any definition of the word.

With a certainty, we already know that "heads" and "tails" are fail parties, representing a "fail" path, and a fail plan. Why on earth would you "vote" for them again? Are you a slow learner?

Again, I do not mean to insult you, but consider this:

If I choose to vote for some crazy radical who wants to take the vote away from women, and re-institute child labor, what difference does it make, if I am the *only* one who does so? As long as two or more citizens have voted *their* conscience, in opposition to mine, for a leader that *they* believe in, *none* of our votes will have been "wasted."

Do you see now? Have you found the "light?"

Maybe "Democracy" *can* work. Maybe if enough of us actually use our "vote" for its intended purpose, we can have a Nation, a society, that is the envy of the world. Once again, we can have the most powerful, vibrant economy in the world. We could have the best roads, schools, bridges, and jobs as well.

Not too long ago, this was the "State of our Union."

My fellow Americans, Plan B will do just that. It will be the first giant step towards the reconstruction of our great Nation.

In the months leading up to the election, do your homework. Participate in this great gift of self-determination, that has been bought and paid for with the blood and tears of the 99% who were before us.

Don't let them down.

Find a local candidate or candidates that you *can* support, that you can believe in. **Just be certain that it is not an incumbent, or any member of "heads" or "tails."** Remember that those two fail parties have broken nearly every promise, and failed at almost every task, and that is why we are on the path of failure today.

In November, when you step into the voting booth to cast your hard-won vote, remember the great struggle it took to get the common person to that place. <u>It was not long ago, that if you were poor, or the wrong color, or the wrong gender, you did not even have the "right" to be in that voting booth at all</u>.

Now you do. What will you do with it? Will you choose to hire the same old failed crew again?

Or will you accept and know with a certainty that you *must* do something different? *You* are responsible, <u>every single one of us is responsible</u>. Everyone who votes for Plan A yet again is choosing to be a part of the problem, not the solution.

For the rest of us, voting for Plan B is the best and proper choice.

It will send a very clear message to the overlords of our society, who think that we are too "ignint," too lazy, too powerless to do anything to help ourselves.

Send them that message. Let them know that they could not possibly be more wrong about the 99%, the heart, the soul, and the backbone of this great Nation.

When *they* wake up, the "morning after" the election, and find themselves "unemployed" like many of us, what will be their "Plan B?"

Thanks for listening.

Part VI

Reconstruction

Once before in the history of our great Nation, we were at an important spiritual crossroads. We had just finished developing a consensus that we were better off as one nation than we were as two, or as many. The price of that decision-making process was huge, both in terms of money, and of lives, blood, and tears.

Our foreign enemies watched and waited for us to destroy ourselves in that conflict, as they hoped we would. They licked their lips in anticipation of reaping the spoils, and robbing the metaphorical corpse of our nation, as some of them do today.

What did we learn from that conflict?

Among other things, we learned that we are our own worst enemies, as we killed each other with much greater efficiency and precision than our external enemies ever did, or have done, to this day. We learned that our Constitution was more than just a piece of paper—it was a sacred idea, an enunciation of greater principles and ideas that were to form and sustain the greatest democratic society in the history of the world.

We learned that our differences were not nearly as great as our similarities, and the conscious decision was made to move forward as a united nation, rather than to dwell on the concepts of punishment and retribution against the "rebellious" factions who had "started" the war.

My fellow Americans, my brothers and sisters, I have invested many words, and many hours in trying to convince you that this is the time and the place to once again make that choice. To put aside the past, and to move forward towards a brighter future for us all. I have talked about "choices" and "plans" and the sale of our Nation to the highest bidders, and I have hoped, even prayed, that I would reach you. Have I done so?

There is no better time than now, there is no better place than here. What are we waiting for? We have the ability to make that quantum leap, that evolutionary shift, as a people and a race. We can move our Nation 100 years ahead of the other nations of the world, in just a few short months.

The will of the people should be enacted in weeks and months, not years or generations. We all have but *one* life, this one. The one we are in *now*, and here. Don't you want the best possible life for yourself, and for your family, your friends, your neighbors? Do you honestly believe that your success must come at the price of causing them to fail? For this is the bill of goods that we have been sold, by the "owners" of our society, the 1%.

That the "perfect" democratic society must somehow resemble a pyramid, with the hordes of the unwashed masses forming the base, and an ever-decreasing number of the fortunate few who have managed to "climb the ladder" of "success" towards the pinnacle.

Do you believe that it is more important to maintain the status quo for the few, than it is to restore the hopes and dreams of *millions*? Are you willing to sacrifice your dreams of a better life so that those few can continue to live *their* dream?

What about your dreams?

How about this one? What would it be like to be debt-free? To no longer be an indentured servant to the overlords of our society?

It is hard to even imagine this condition of being, because we have existed this way for so long, it has become a way of life. Our children have come to accept it as well. They have acknowledged that their future will also consist of debt and servitude, and they no longer expect that they will surpass us, their parents, and would be content to simply live as well as we do, no worse.

What happened to our "American Dream?" Is it still alive somewhere, in you? In your neighbors, in your friends?

I believe that it is.

So strongly do I believe this, that I have spent many hours of my life, and many dollars from my pocket to construct and deliver these essays to you, the 99%. It is my hope, *my* dream, that I will reach at least *some* of you, that you will look inside yourself and see what I see, that is, a glorious future for this great Nation, and for its people.

That you will look into the eyes of your children, and see what I have seen, the innocent and perhaps naïve hope that things can be better, that they *will* be better, and that you and I have the means and the desire to enact that change.

We have the technology. We have all the tools and supplies that we need. We can build a better, more perfect society for ourselves and our children.

We have the ideas, the strength, the heart, and even the desire.

The only thing we lack is *faith*. That is what the "American Dream" is all about.

It is about "belief." When we decide that we will achieve something, we do. We can change the face of this Nation, and indeed the entire world, should we choose to do so. We could build a sea-level canal through Mexico, irrigate the entire continent of Africa, and even colonize the Moon, if we set our minds to it and believed that we could.

We could eradicate disease, extend the human lifespan to 100 years and beyond, and ensure that no child ever went to sleep hungry at night in one city, while perfectly edible, nutritious food is buried in a landfill in another.

What are your dreams?

Do you remember them? Think back with me, to a time perhaps not long ago, when you graduated from college, or high school, and you were filled with visions of a bright future for yourself and your eventual family. When you were naïve enough to believe that things would just somehow "work out" for the better, whether or not you took any specific action.

That time has passed. That ship has sailed.

Today is a new day, in a new place, at a new time.

Now is the perfect time to take action to reconstruct the dreams of your youth. To restore the dreams of your children. Remember that when they look into *your* eyes, and see nothing but hopelessness and despair, that this is the example you are setting for them. This is the expectation you are setting. *You* must have hopes and dreams if you are to teach your children to do the same.

I believe that those who contribute more *to* society should receive more rewards *from* society.

I believe that those rewards should be immediate and visible to all, as exemplars to others of the benefit to the self and society that good citizenship brings to the Nation.

For example, we are rich enough that we could and should have quarterly "festivals" in celebration of our good fortune and our accomplishments as a people. Two or even three-day national events, filled with food, drink, fun, and entertainment, paid for by the hard work of the people, and open to all who have fulfilled the requirements of "good citizenship."

During these festivals, the ideas and innovations of undiscovered artists, musicians, writers, scientists, and all "dreamers" could be showcased and displayed to the public eye, and even "liked" and "shared" across the nation. This process would help ensure that the voice of the people is heard, and it would instantly help determine where scarce national resources should be allocated. Quarterly, monthly, or even weekly "opinion" polls of the citizens could be used to measure their satisfaction with the current path of government and its respective leaders, all recorded instantly and uploaded anonymously, in real time.

We have the technology to accomplish all of this**, yet who amongst our failed "heads" and "tails" parties, led by geriatric millionaires, is even talking to you about such things, as I am?** Their only real concern seems to be in maintaining their own positions at the top of the aforementioned pyramid, and protecting the status quo of their masters and peers as well.

Our needs and concerns, the concerns of "the people" of this nation, without whom there would be no "Nation," do not even register for them. They are not even a matter for discussion, as they sit and take their ease, comfortable in their palaces and high places.

For now, they are smug and secure, but let us take that security away from them. Let us put *them* out on the street. Let us cut the top right off of that failed pyramidal structure they have built upon the backs of us, the 99%, the heart, the soul, and the backbone of this great Nation.

Let us establish the programs and rules of law that *we* decide matter to us, and let us remove those we do not desire. **Let us do these things immediately**, not at some unknown time perhaps eventually in the future. Let us remove and replace any and all of our so-called leaders who do not enact our will, quickly and efficiently.

We should destroy and rebuild all of the failed institutions of our society, beginning with the political structure, and not stopping until we have reformed *everything*.

Education

Law Enforcement

Taxation

Public Works and Infrastructure

Foreign Policy

Health Care

Defense

All are in serious need of reconstruction and reform, and all are seemingly ignored by the overlords of our society, except when it is beneficial to their particular election or re-election campaign—then quickly forgotten, of course, the "morning after," once the desired outcome of that deception has been achieved.

We should be soliciting and accepting the ideas and dreams of all the productive members of our society, not just those fortunate enough by accident of birth to have enough money to pay for the right to be heard. We have the technology to do this, in real time, every single day. We can process data as no other nation or society was ever able to do before, yet we continue to run this country as if this were the 18th century, not the 21st.

As I have asked you before, why might this be? Who benefits more from the perpetual continuation of the antique path of failure? More importantly, who stands to gain the most from its destruction?

The answer to that third question is the most obvious and important one.

Why, we do, of course. We the 99%, that is.

This is *our* country.

Let's take it back, and make it in our own image.

Thanks for listening.

Part VII

Class Warfare

There comes a time, when the people of a nation have been oppressed for too long, with no hope of reprieve, that a consensus is finally reached among them that there is no other alternative than to take immediate action against their abusers.

The "owners" of our society have bought and paid for the political process that now ensures the continuity of their rule. There is no longer even the "pretense" of the opportunity for public service by anyone who might actually have the desire and the motivation to be just that—a "servant" of the people, not a "master" of them. The 1% have effectively established themselves as the hereditary rulers of this nation, a concept that was absolutely abhorrent to the Founders.

This usurpation of the democratic will of the people is so pervasive, so entrenched, and so lethal to the spirit of the Nation that it now demands a response by those who love their country, their people, and their American way of life. There is no more time for inaction. To do nothing is not a viable option any more. We must *not* fiddle while our "Rome" burns.

Complacency is complicity.

Both are absolutely unacceptable.

The 99%, it seems, have already been at war for quite some time now, we just had not yet realized it. The war was started by the 1%, *not* the 99, and it has been waged for over a generation already. No "formal" declaration was ever made, but the outcome of this "war of attrition" has been as destructive to "We the People" as any other in our great history as a Nation, if not more so.

The reduction of our people to second-class status versus the other nations of the world, and the subsequent diminishment of our craftsmanship, pride, and national spirit, such as that we no longer aspire to "greatness," but merely "mediocrity," speaks volumes in and of itself, and is the greatest crime of all.

The selling and mortgaging of our future and our dreams to our foreign enemies is in progress as I write, and continues in full-force, as "we" seem unable to manage our own economic house and Ship of State. In the previous *Essays for the 99%*, I laid out the case against the established ruling order of our society, in great detail. (See parts II and III, particularly).

Once again, we must look to the past, as we prepare for the future. The 1% have successfully destroyed our present hopes and dreams, and we must, must, *must* not let them destroy our future as well. To do so would be a betrayal of our children, our way of life, and would be an abandonment of the

"American Dream." We simply cannot allow this to continue, and therefore:

When in the Course of human events, it becomes necessary for one people to dissolve the political bands which have connected them with another, and to assume among the powers of the earth, the separate and equal station to which the Laws of Nature and of Nature's God entitle them, **a decent respect to the opinions of mankind requires that they should declare the causes which impel them to the separation.**

Regarding those causes, I propose that (among others) the 1% have committed the following crimes and offenses against us:

For refusing to honor the will of the people, and refusing assent to laws necessary for the public good.

For setting aside those rules of law that the people *have* established, in accordance with their Democratic will, in direct violation of the *Constitution* and the *Bill of Rights*.

For giving aid and comfort to our Foreign Enemies, by selling and mortgaging the Nation's assets, held in trust for the people, without their consent.

I have stated only a few of their violations of the public trust, but the list of their offenses goes on and on, yet the willingness of our "leaders" to address them seems to fade at an alarming rate, as each successive generation of the "hereditary rulers" of our nation appears less and less concerned with the welfare of the People, and cares only for their own comfort and security, and that of their masters and peers.

As I have said before, when you betray your friends, your family, your neighbors for nothing more than money, then you are clearly, simply, and *only* a traitor. While our current "rule of law" does provide for the proper punishment of such offenders, in the interest of compassion I propose leniency. That in exchange for the forfeiture of their ill-gotten gains, (which were extracted from the people anyway) they are allowed, even "encouraged" to leave this great Nation, to which they obviously have no allegiance, loyalty, or fealty anyway, as evidenced by their repeated offenses. Those actions truly speak much louder than words, and their abuses continue unabated, as detailed in previous *Essays*.

As great as the contributions of the 1% are, to the betterment of the race, the country, and indeed the entirety of our species, surely there must be multitudes of other nations that are clamoring for these shining examples of the human spirit to grace their shores.

They should have little difficulty finding homes and comfort amidst the warm embraces of those foreign enemies to whom they have sold or given so much already, correct? Therefore I say, "Good riddance, and good luck to you!" as we bid them farewell and safe journey to their new, more welcoming homes, amid a people who will recognize and acknowledge their natural prerogative to demand submission and authority over those lesser peoples, granted by Divine Right, and the virtue of the accumulation of wealth as a means to its own end.

Why should we offer continued comfort and security to those who have declared war upon us? A class of people who have as much as clearly stated that their goal is the reduction of our status to that of the beleaguered feudal serf, indebted to his masters for *the entirety of his life*, with no hope of liberation from his condition? That his children are expected to embrace a perpetual condition of poverty and servitude as well?

How can loaning money to your own people at rates of 30% or *more* be anything *but* a snare for them? A trap meant to imprison them forever in a cycle of debt and poverty? This while "our" government (owned by the 1%, of course) loans *them* that same money at 1% or *less*. Think about this for a moment. Is this "fair" or "equitable?" Who does "the government's" money belong to? *Some* of the people, or *all* of them? Talk about a conflict of "interest." If some can borrow money for free or practically so, then all should be able to.

Imagine if you could "refinance" all of your household's debt—house payments, car payments, credit cards, student loans, etc. at 1% or even 0%. How much more room in the family budget would there be, from one moment to the next? **It is somehow "offensive" to our masters to do this for us, but perfectly acceptable to "lend" our money to their friends and country club buddies for "free**," while they then turn around and *loan us our own money at 30%!*

Of course, this process ensures that the "cycle of poverty" continues unabated, and that many of us will remain "indentured servants" *forever*.

Because of these and other destructive policies that the 1% have perpetrated upon us, in less than a generation, we have gone from a net "asset" nation to a net "debtor" nation. Our masters now think of us as nothing more than cogs in their brutal machine, to be exploited until "used up," as any other "resource" is.

Is that how *you* think of your children? Your neighbors, your friends, your family? As nothing more than "commodities" to be discarded when no longer useful or profitable? Is this the future that you dreamed for them?

If so, please stop reading now.

You will only torment yourself further, as your internal conflict with being an honorary "poor" member of the 1% tears at your insides. It pains me to speak of it, but there is nothing funnier or more pathetic to me than a poverty-stricken "Republican," who has *nothing,* not even shoes on her children's feet, as she staunchly advocates for the right of her masters to take *everything* (including those shoes) from them.

If you have nothing, then you have nothing to lose. They have taken it all, already.

So stand up, for a change. Get off your knees, and onto your feet.

Declare your own war on the 1%, the traitors of our Nation, our culture, our way of life.

You certainly do not owe them any allegiance, or loyalty.

For they have none to you.

They are perfectly content to see your despair, they will show you no mercy, no compassion. They will not redress the harm they have caused you. Your future means *nothing* to them.

Why should theirs mean anything to *you?*

I know, I know. You are a Christian, or a person of another faith, a believer in forgiveness and redemption.

As am I.

This is why I proposed exile, and not the fate that these traitors deserve, by rule of law.

Once we have taken the necessary steps to help ourselves, the future will immediately become much brighter, if only because the "dark cloud" of oppression will have been lifted from us.

We are better than this. That we have to concern ourselves with our own survival, at risk from *those enemies within our own society*, speaks volumes, does it not?

How can we prepare to face our foreign enemies, if we are usurped and destroyed from within, by that lethal virus that infects us, the 1%? These pathetic excuses for human beings that have no allegiance to God, to us, to country, to anyone or anything but *Money*.

Is it even possible to be rich, noble, *and* patriotic? Of course it is. History is filled with examples of such honorable men and women, rare as they may be.

Benjamin Guggenheim said: (As he prepared to die a brutal watery death during the Titanic disaster).

"We are prepared to go down like gentlemen . . . . *No* woman shall be left aboard this ship because Ben Guggenheim was a coward."

Awesome.

Wow. Such nobility! Here was a man, an *extremely* wealthy man, faced with the spectre of his own imminent death, who could have chosen a number of less noble paths to his own salvation, who instead counted himself amongst the "common" man, that his place in life might be taken by a "poor woman."

To all of our sisters, wives, and daughters, imagine yourselves aboard the "Ship of State" with millionaires "A, B, C, and D," who propose to "lead" and "represent" you today. Which of them, do you suppose, would offer you *their* place in the lifeboat?"

Any of them?

To the contrary, these so-called "leaders" would quickly toss you out, and gladly take your place.

Do you believe that there are any such noble individuals amongst the 1% now?

I do.

A very few. Those who *have* stood up and said, "I have enough. I love my country, my people, and I want to give back to them."

They know who they are, and yes, we know who *you* are, you blessed few. We shall not account you amongst the wicked, when the reckoning is made. Your children will also be counted as worthy, because you cared to speak out, even though it did not "profit" you to do so.

For the rest of you, those foul and putrid excuses for human "life" we are subjected to now as the leaders and "owners" of our society and our Nation, there will be no mercy, no compassion, in this life or the next. You *will* be held accountable for all of your crimes. Fair warning has been given.

Let the few gems amongst the great coal heap of the 1% take this opportunity to stand up now, and declare your allegiance to this great Nation and its people, the 99% of us who are the heart, the soul, and the backbone of it. You owe us loyalty and respect.

Show it now, or make your "travel arrangements," while you still can.

The anger of the people becomes rage, and rage begets violence, and violence seeks an outlet.

Ultimately, we will take back what is ours, by any means "necessary."

Thanks for listening.

Afterword

The original text that was to become the *Essays for the 99%*, Parts I and II was written back in 2009, obviously before the "Occupy" movement.

So essentially I was writing for an audience that did not yet exist as an "organized" group.

The thought process that was to form *The Carrot and The Stick*, and *A Call to Action*, began to gestate during my college years, ironically enough, back at UC Davis, sight of the infamous "pepper spraying" act of terrorism against the peaceful protesters.

You could say that I saw the "writing on the wall," as I watched the decline of "The People" and their interests for the entirety of my adult life.

I watched our wages decline as prices increased, watched our jobs being exported, our country mortgaged, our future traded to our foreign enemies for the proverbial "30 pieces of silver."

Ultimately I could no longer contain the words that I had long spoken to anyone who would listen, and decided to commit them to the printed and digital page.

If I fail to inspire, to motivate, to germinate reform, at least history will know that *We the People* of this once greater Nation did *not* silently acquiesce to this "violation" of our American Dream.

We spoke out, we protested, we "ranted" to all who would listen, (and many who would not) as we tried to preserve the idea of a "United Nation."

If you have read the entire series of the *Essays for the 99%*, you will see the evolution of my thought process from a position of pure outrage in Parts I and II, to a more philosophical and calm approach to the awful betrayal we are now subjected to.

Parts III through VII were written over a three-month span in late 2011, early 2012, so about three years after what was to become the first two parts.

Will there be more *Essays for the 99%*?

Possibly.

Should there be?

Definitely.

I have outlined several more already, but when I reach a place where I am simply repeating myself, that will be the natural stopping point, of course.

Part VIII is fomenting now, and is tentatively entitled M.O.T.S, or *More of the Same*, which is what we can expect if we do nothing to change the path that we are on.

More joblessness, while our "leaders" crow about adding millions of "minimum wage" jobs, more foreclosures while they trumpet "recovery," and more abuse of the people's rights as the 1% shout "Freedom!" from their palaces and high places.

You don't have to "buy" the *Essays for the 99%* in order to hear their message. You can listen to a *free* author's read at the website:

johndavidauthor.com

The Auction and *The Choice* are available for free in all ebook formats, and you can download the PDF as well.

By the way, I don't expect *anyone* to agree with *everything* I say. Whether you agree or disagree, please add your voice to the debate. There is no more time for inaction.

Complacency is complicity, and both are absolutely unacceptable.

Thanks for listening.

-John

Made in the USA
Middletown, DE
25 October 2020